Greatest Ever

Chocolate

The All Time Top 20 Greatest Recipes

Greatest Ever

Chocolate

The All Time Top 20 Greatest Recipes

p

This is a Parragon Book
First published in 2002

Parragon
Queen Street House
4 Queen Street
Bath BA1 1HE, UK

ISBN: 0-75256-851-5

Printed in China

NOTE

This book uses metric and imperial measurements. Follow the same
units of measurement throughout; do not mix metric and imperial.
All spoon measurements are level: teaspoons are assumed to be 5 ml,
and tablespoons are assumed to be 15 ml. Unless otherwise stated,
milk is assumed to be full fat, eggs and individual vegetables such as
potatoes are medium, and pepper is freshly ground black pepper.

The times given for each recipe are an approximate guide only
because the preparation times may differ according to the techniques
used by different people and the cooking times may vary as a result
of the type of oven used. The preparation times include the chilling
times, where appropriate.

Recipes using raw or very lightly cooked eggs should be
avoided by infants, the elderly, pregnant women, convalescents,
and anyone suffering from an illness.

CONTENTS

INTRODUCTION

Go on, spoil yourself with one of life's affordable luxuries – chocolate! Here is a selection of some of the most luscious chocolate cakes and biscuits, a wickedly rich cheesecake, some melt-in-the-mouth profiteroles and sweet fudge. These delicious chocolate desserts are guaranteed to cheer you up whenever a chocolate craving strikes, at any time of the day or night.

STORAGE

Store chocolate in a cool, dry place, away from direct heat or sunlight. Most chocolate can be stored for about 1 year. When keeping it in a refrigerator, make sure that it is well wrapped to prevent it picking up flavours from other foods. Keep chocolate decorations in airtight containers, interleaved with sheets of non-stick baking paper. Dark chocolate will keep for 4 weeks this way, and white chocolate for 2 weeks.

Right: Versatile chocolate is suitable for everything from elaborate cakes to small morsels such as truffles.

WHAT IS CHOCOLATE?

Chocolate is processed from the bean of the cacao tree. This tree originated in South America but now grows in Africa, the West Indies, the tropical parts of America and the Far East.

Cacao beans develop in large pods. Once harvested both pods and beans are allowed to dry and ferment in the sun. The pod's pulp evaporates and the bean's chocolatey flavour develops.

The outer skin is then removed and the beans are either left in the sun for a little longer or put into ovens to roast. Finally the beans are shelled and the kernels are used for making cocoa and chocolate.

Below: The lightness of fresh fruit is an ideal complement to the rich flavour of chocolate.

Processing the kernels

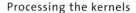

Cacao bean kernels are ground and processed to produce a thick mixture or paste called cocoa solids. It is the cocoa solid content which is used to gauge the quality of the chocolate. The cocoa solids are pressed to remove some of the fat – the cocoa butter. They are then further processed to produce the rich substance known and loved as chocolate.

TYPES OF CHOCOLATE

Dark chocolate

This contains anything from 30 to 75 per cent cocoa solids. It has a slightly bittersweet flavour and dark colour. It is the chocolate most used in cooking. For everyday cooking and the majority of recipes calling for dark chocolate, use one with about 50 per cent cocoa solids.

Dark chocolate with a higher cocoa solid content will give a richer, more intense flavour. Often called luxury or continental chocolate, it has a cocoa solid content of 70 to 75 per cent and is the most expensive. Chocolate recipes usually indicate when it is essential to use the best chocolate.

Milk chocolate

As its name suggests, this chocolate contains milk and has a lovely creamy, mild, sweet flavour. It is mostly used as an eating chocolate rather than in cooking.

However, it does have its place in chocolate cookery, especially for decorations and when a milder, creamy flavour is required. It is more sensitive to heat than dark chocolate, so extra care must be taken when melting it.

White chocolate

This has a lower cocoa butter and cocoa solids content than other chocolate. It can be temperamental when used in cooking. Always choose a luxury white cooking chocolate to minimize the risks and take great care not to overheat when melting it. Although it does not have a particularly distinctive chocolate flavour, white chocolate is useful for colour contrast, especially when decorating chocolate cakes.

Couverture

Although this is the chocolate preferred by professionals because it retains a high gloss after melting and cooling, it requires tempering (carefully monitored heating and cooling). It is only available from specialist suppliers and therefore has not been used in this book.

Chocolate chips

These are available in dark, milk and white chocolate, and are used for baking and cake decoration.

Chocolate-flavoured cake covering

This inferior product is scorned by true chocolate lovers. However, its high fat content makes it easier to handle when making some decorations, such as curls. If you want to retain the flavour of high quality chocolate, but make it easier to work with, you can compromise by adding a few squares of chocolate-flavoured cake covering to a good quality dark chocolate.

Cocoa powder

This is the powder left after the cocoa butter has been pressed from the roasted and ground cocoa beans. It is unsweetened and bitter in flavour. It gives a good dark colour and strong chocolate flavour when used in baking.

dark chocolate

milk chocolate

Right: Chocolate varies in colour and sweetness according to its cocoa solid content.

white chocolate

9

Before you start making any of the chocolate treats in this book, you will need to know the basics of chocolate-melting techniques.

WORKING WITH CHOCOLATE

Melting chocolate

Do not melt chocolate in a pan over direct heat unless you are melting it with other ingredients, such as butter or syrup – even then, the temperature should be kept very low.

Break the chocolate into small, equal-sized pieces and put them in a heatproof bowl. Sit the bowl over a pan of gently simmering water, making sure that the base of the bowl is clear of the water. Once the chocolate starts to melt, stir gently until smooth. If necessary, leave over the simmering water for a little longer. Make sure that no drops of water come into contact with the molten chocolate or it will solidify.

To melt the chocolate in a microwave, break the chocolate into small pieces and place in a microwave-proof bowl. Timing will vary according to the type and

dark chocolate pieces

chocolate chips

mixing bowl

quantity of chocolate. As a guide, 125 g/4½ oz dark chocolate takes 2 minutes on High to melt; white or milk chocolate takes 2–3 minutes on Medium.

When the time is up, stir the chocolate and leave to stand for a few minutes before stirring again. If necessary, return the bowl to the microwave for a further 30 seconds.

wooden spoon

spatula

Setting chocolate

Chocolate sets best at 18°C/65°F, although it will set more slowly in a slightly warmer room. If set in the refrigerator it may develop a white bloom and be very brittle. If possible, set chocolate decorations in a cool room.

Right: For a quick chocolate fix, drinks can be whipped up in just a few minutes.

CHOCOLATE MOUSSE

›Serves 8   ›Preparation time: 2¼ hours   ›Cooking time: 5 minutes

INGREDIENTS

100 g/3½ oz dark chocolate, melted

300 ml/10 fl oz natural yogurt

150 ml/5 fl oz Quark

4 tbsp caster sugar

1 tbsp orange juice

1 tbsp brandy

1½ tsp gelatine

140 ml/4½ fl oz cold water

2 large egg whites

coarsely grated dark and white chocolate and orange zest, to decorate

METHOD

1 Put the melted chocolate, natural yogurt, Quark, caster sugar, orange juice and brandy in a food processor and blend for 30 seconds. Transfer the mixture to a large bowl.

2 Sprinkle the gelatine over the water and stir until dissolved.

3 In a small saucepan, bring the gelatine and water to the boil for 2 minutes. Leave to cool slightly, then stir into the chocolate mixture.

4 Whisk the egg whites until stiff peaks form and fold into the chocolate mixture using a metal spoon.

5 Line an 850-ml/1½-pint loaf tin with clingfilm. Spoon the mousse into the tin. Chill for 2 hours in the refrigerator, or until set. Turn the mousse out on to a plate, decorate with grated chocolate and orange zest and serve.

RICH CHOCOLATE PUDDING

>Serves 6   >Preparation time: 10–15 minutes   >Cooking time: 1½–2 hours

INGREDIENTS

SPONGE

150 g/5½ oz soft margarine

150 g/5½ oz self-raising flour

150 g/5½ oz golden syrup

3 eggs

25 g/1 oz cocoa powder

CHOCOLATE FUDGE SAUCE

100 g/3½ oz dark chocolate

125 ml/4 fl oz condensed milk

4 tbsp double cream

METHOD

1 Lightly grease a 1.2-litre/2-pint pudding basin.

2 Place the ingredients for the sponge in a mixing bowl and beat until smooth.

3 Spoon into the prepared basin and level the top. Cover with a disc of baking paper and tie a pleated sheet of foil over the basin. Steam for 1½–2 hours, or until the pudding is cooked and springy to the touch.

4 To make the sauce, break the chocolate into small pieces and place in a small pan with the condensed milk. Heat gently, stirring, until the chocolate melts.

5 Remove the pan from the heat and stir in the double cream.

6 To serve the pudding, turn it out on to a serving plate and pour over a little of the chocolate fudge sauce. Serve the remaining sauce separately.

CHOCOLATE CARAMEL SQUARES

>Makes 12 >Preparation time: 55 minutes >Cooking time: 30 minutes

INGREDIENTS
175 g/6 oz plain flour

125 g/4½ oz butter, cut into small pieces

50 g/1¾ oz soft brown sugar, sieved

TOPPING
4 tbsp butter

50 g/1¾ oz soft brown sugar

400 ml/14 fl oz condensed milk

150 g/5½ oz milk chocolate

METHOD
1 Grease a 23-cm/9-inch square cake tin.

2 Sieve the flour into a mixing bowl and rub in the butter with your fingers until the mixture resembles fine breadcrumbs. Add the sugar and mix to form a firm dough.

3 Press the dough into the bottom of the prepared tin and prick all over with a fork.

4 Bake in a preheated oven, 190°C/375°F/Gas Mark 5, for 20 minutes, or until lightly golden. Leave to cool in the tin.

5 To make the topping, place the butter, sugar and condensed milk in a non-stick saucepan and cook over a gentle heat, stirring constantly, until the mixture comes to the boil.

6 Reduce the heat and cook for 4–5 minutes, or until the caramel is pale golden and thick and is coming away from the sides of the pan. Pour the topping over the shortbread base and leave to cool.

7 When the caramel topping is firm, melt the milk chocolate and spread it over the topping. Leave to set in a cool place, then cut the shortbread into squares or fingers to serve.

DARK CHOCOLATE TORTE

> Serves 10 > Preparation time: 1 hour 25 minutes > Cooking time: 40–45 minutes

INGREDIENTS

225 g/8 oz dark chocolate, broken into pieces

3 tbsp water

150 g/5½ oz soft brown sugar

175 g/6 oz butter, softened

25 g/1 oz ground almonds

3 tbsp self-raising flour

5 eggs, separated

100 g/3½ oz blanched almonds,
finely chopped

icing sugar, for dusting

fresh fruit, such as strawberries and
blueberries, to serve (optional)

METHOD

1 Grease a 23-cm/9-inch loose-based cake tin
or line with baking paper.

2 In a saucepan set over a very low heat, melt
the chocolate with the water, stirring until
smooth. Add the brown sugar and stir until
dissolved, taking the pan off the heat to
prevent it overheating.

3 Add the butter in small amounts until it has
melted into the chocolate. Remove from the
heat and lightly stir in the ground almonds
and flour. Add the egg yolks one at a time,
beating well after each addition.

4 In a large mixing bowl, whisk the egg whites
until they stand in soft peaks, then fold them
into the chocolate mixture with a metal spoon.
Stir in the chopped almonds. Pour the mixture
into the tin and level the surface.

5 Bake in a preheated oven, 180°C/ 350°F/Gas
Mark 4, for 40–45 minutes, or until well risen
and firm (the cake will crack on the surface
during cooking).

6 Leave the cake to cool in the tin for
30–40 minutes, then turn it out on to a wire
rack to cool completely. Dust with icing sugar
and serve in slices with fresh fruit, if using.

MIXED FRUIT FLORENTINES

> Makes 40   > Preparation time: 30 minutes   > Cooking time: 15 minutes

INGREDIENTS

6 tbsp butter

75 g/2¾ oz caster sugar

25 g/1 oz sultanas or raisins

25 g/1 oz glacé cherries, chopped

25 g/1 oz crystallised ginger, chopped

25 g/1 oz sunflower seeds

100 g/3½ oz flaked almonds

2 tbsp double cream

175 g/6 oz dark or milk chocolate

METHOD

1 Lightly grease and flour 2 baking trays or line with baking paper. Place the butter in a small pan and heat gently until melted. Add the sugar, stir until dissolved, then bring the mixture to the boil. Remove from the heat and stir in the sultanas or raisins, cherries, ginger, sunflower seeds and almonds. Mix well, then beat in the cream.

2 Place small teaspoons of the fruit and nut mixture on to the prepared baking tray, allowing space for the mixture to spread. Bake in a preheated oven, 180°C/350°F/Gas Mark 4, for 10–12 minutes, or until light golden.

3 Remove from the oven and, while still hot, use a round biscuit cutter to pull in the edges of each florentine to form a perfect round. Leave to cool and crispen before removing from the baking tray.

4 Melt most of the chocolate and spread it on a sheet of baking paper. When it is on the point of setting, place the biscuits flat-side down on the chocolate and leave to harden.

5 Cut around the florentines and remove from the paper. Spread a little more chocolate on the already coated side of the florentines and use a fork to mark waves in the chocolate. Leave to set. Arrange the florentines on a plate with alternate sides facing upwards. Keep cool.

REFRIGERATOR SQUARES

➤Makes 16   ➤Preparation time: 2¼ hours   ➤Cooking time: 5 minutes

INGREDIENTS

275 g/9½ oz dark chocolate

175 g/6 oz butter

4 tbsp golden syrup

2 tbsp dark rum, optional

175 g/6 oz plain biscuits, such as Rich Tea

25 g/1 oz toasted rice cereal

50 g/1¼ oz chopped walnuts or pecan nuts

100 g/3½ oz glacé cherries,
roughly chopped

25 g/1 oz white chocolate, to decorate

METHOD

1 Place the dark chocolate in a large mixing bowl with the butter, syrup and rum, if using, and set over a saucepan of gently simmering water until melted, stirring until blended.

2 Break the biscuits into small pieces and stir into the chocolate mixture along with the rice cereal, nuts and cherries.

3 Line an 18-cm/7-inch square cake tin with baking paper. Pour the mixture into the tin and level the top, pressing down well with the back of a spoon. Chill for 2 hours.

4 To decorate, melt the white chocolate and drizzle it over the top of the cake in a random pattern. Leave to set. To serve, carefully turn out of the tin and remove the baking paper. Cut into 16 squares.

CHOCOLATE CAKE WITH CITRUS FROSTING

>Serves 8 >Preparation time: 1 hour >Cooking time: 30 minutes

INGREDIENTS

100 g/3½ oz dark chocolate

250 g/9 oz self-raising flour

1 tsp bicarbonate of soda

225 g/8 oz butter

400 g/14 oz dark muscovado sugar

1 tsp vanilla essence

3 eggs

125 ml/4 fl oz buttermilk

225 ml/8 fl oz boiling water

candied orange peel, to decorate

FROSTING

300 g/10½ oz caster sugar

2 egg whites

1 tbsp lemon juice

3 tbsp orange juice

METHOD

1 Lightly grease two 20-cm/8-inch shallow round cake tins and line the bases. Melt the chocolate. Sieve the flour and bicarbonate of soda together.

2 Beat the butter and sugar in a bowl until pale and fluffy. Add in the vanilla essence and the eggs, one at a time, beating well after each addition. Add a little flour if the mixture begins to curdle.

3 Fold the melted chocolate into the mixture. Gradually fold in the remaining flour, then stir in the buttermilk and boiling water.

4 Divide the mixture between the tins and level the tops. Bake in a preheated oven, 190°C/375°F/Gas Mark 5, for 30 minutes, or until springy to the touch. Leave to cool in the tin for 5 minutes, then transfer to a wire rack to cool completely.

5 Place the frosting ingredients in a large bowl set over a pan of gently simmering water. Whisk with electric beaters until thickened and forming soft peaks. Remove from the heat and whisk until the mixture is cool.

6 Sandwich the 2 cakes together with a little of the frosting, then spread the remainder over the sides and top of the cake, swirling it as you do so. Decorate with the candied orange peel.

FROSTED CHOCOLATE BUTTER CAKE

>Serves 8–12   >Preparation time: 1 hour   >Cooking time: 30–35 minutes

INGREDIENTS

4 eggs

125 g/4½ oz caster sugar

125 g/4½ oz plain flour

1 tbsp cocoa powder

2 tbsp butter, melted

75 g/2¾ oz dark chocolate, melted

150 g/5½ oz finely chopped walnuts

walnut halves, to decorate

ICING

75 g/2¾ oz dark chocolate

125 g/4½ oz butter

200 g/7 oz icing sugar

2 tbsp milk

METHOD

1 Grease an 18-cm/7-inch deep round cake tin and line the base. Place the eggs and caster sugar in a mixing bowl and whisk with electric beaters for 10 minutes, or until the mixture is light and foamy and the whisk leaves a trail that lasts a few seconds when lifted.

2 Sieve together the flour and cocoa powder and fold in with a metal spoon or spatula. Fold in the melted butter and chocolate, and the chopped walnuts. Pour into the prepared tin and bake in a preheated oven, 160°C/325°F/ Gas Mark 3, and bake for 30–35 minutes, or until springy to the touch.

3 Leave to cool in the tin for 5 minutes, then transfer to a wire rack to cool completely. Cut the cold cake into 2 layers.

4 To make the icing, melt the dark chocolate and leave to cool slightly. Beat together the butter, icing sugar and milk in a bowl until the mixture is pale and fluffy, then whisk in the melted chocolate.

5 Sandwich the 2 cake layers with some of the icing and place on a serving plate. Spread the remaining icing over the top of the cake with a palette knife, swirling it slightly. Decorate the cake with the walnut halves and serve.

CHOCOLATE ÉCLAIRS

›Makes 10 ›Preparation time: 45 minutes ›Cooking time: 45–50 minutes

INGREDIENTS

CHOUX PASTRY

150 ml/5 fl oz water

4 tbsp butter, cut into small pieces

85 g/3 oz strong plain flour, sieved

2 eggs

PATISSERIE CREAM

2 eggs, lightly beaten

50 g/1¾ oz caster sugar

2 tbsp cornflour

300 ml/10 fl oz milk

¼ tsp vanilla essence

ICING

2 tbsp butter

1 tbsp milk

1 tbsp cocoa powder

100 g/3½ oz icing sugar

a little white chocolate, melted

METHOD

1 Lightly grease a baking tray. To make the choux pastry, place the water in a pan, add the butter and heat until melted. Bring to a rolling boil, then remove from the heat and add the flour in one go, beating well until the mixture leaves the sides of the pan and forms a ball. Allow to cool slightly.

2 Gradually beat in the eggs to form a smooth, glossy mixture. Spoon into a large piping bag fitted with a 1-cm/½-inch plain nozzle.

3 Sprinkle the baking tray with a little water. Pipe éclairs 7.5 cm/3 inches long, spaced well apart. Bake in a preheated oven, 200°C/400°F/ Gas Mark 6, for 30–35 minutes, or until crisp and golden. Make a small slit in each one to let the steam escape, then cool on a rack.

4 To make the patisserie cream, whisk the eggs and sugar until thick and creamy, then fold in the cornflour. Heat the milk until almost boiling and pour on to the eggs, whisking. Transfer to a pan and cook over a low heat, stirring until thick. Remove from the heat and stir in the vanilla essence. Cover with baking paper and cool.

5 To make the icing, melt the butter with the milk in a pan, remove from the heat and stir in the cocoa and sugar.

6 Split the éclairs lengthways and pipe in the patisserie cream. Spread the icing over the top of the éclairs, then quickly spoon over the melted white chocolate and swirl in. Leave to set before serving.

WHITE CHOCOLATE CREAM CAKE

>Serves 10 >Preparation time: 1¼ hours >Cooking time: 35–40 minutes

INGREDIENTS

75 g/2¾ oz dark chocolate

4 eggs

100 g/3½ oz cup caster sugar

100 g/3½ oz plain flour

DARK CHOCOLATE CREAM

300 ml/10 fl oz double cream

150 g/5½ oz dark chocolate, broken into small pieces

WHITE CHOCOLATE ICING

75 g/2¾ oz white chocolate

1 tbsp butter

1 tbsp milk

50 g/1¼ oz icing sugar

METHOD

1 To prepare the chocolate caraque to top the cake, melt the dark chocolate and spread it on a marble or acrylic board. As it sets, pull a knife across it quickly at a 45° angle to make curls. Chill in the refrigerator until needed.

2 Grease a 20-cm/8-inch round springform tin and line the base.

3 Whisk the eggs and caster sugar in a large mixing bowl with electric beaters for about 10 minutes, until the mixture is light and foamy and the whisk leaves a trail that lasts a few seconds when lifted.

4 Sieve the flour and fold in with a metal spoon. Pour into the prepared tin. Bake in a preheated oven, 180°C/350°F/Gas Mark 4, for 35–40 minutes, or until springy to the touch. Leave to cool slightly, then transfer to a wire rack to cool completely. Cut into 2 layers.

5 To make the chocolate cream, place the cream in a saucepan and bring to the boil, stirring. Add the chocolate and stir until melted. Remove from the heat and leave to cool. Beat with a wooden spoon until thick.

6 Sandwich the 2 cake layers together with the chocolate cream and place on a wire rack.

7 To make the icing, melt the chocolate and butter together, stirring. Whisk in the milk and sugar. Continue whisking until the icing is cool, then use it to coat the cake. Decorate with the chilled chocolate caraque and leave to set.

MARBLED CHOCOLATE LOAF

> Serves 10 > Preparation time: 50 minutes > Cooking time: 30 minutes

INGREDIENTS

175 g/6 oz caster sugar

175 g/6 oz soft margarine

½ tsp vanilla essence

3 eggs

225 g/8 oz self-raising flour, sieved

50 g/1¾ oz dark chocolate

icing sugar, to dust

METHOD

1 Lightly grease a 450-g/1-lb loaf tin.

2 Beat together the sugar and soft margarine in a bowl until light and fluffy.

3 Beat in the vanilla essence. Gradually add the eggs, beating well after each addition. Carefully fold in the self-raising flour.

4 Divide the mixture in half. Melt the dark chocolate and stir into one half of the mixture until well combined.

5 Place the vanilla mixture in the tin and level the top. Spread the chocolate layer over the vanilla layer.

6 Bake in a preheated oven, 190°C/375°F/ Gas Mark 5, for 30 minutes, or until springy to the touch.

7 Leave the loaf to cool in the tin for a few minutes before transferring to a wire rack to cool completely.

8 Serve dusted with icing sugar.

YULE LOG

> Serves 8–10 > Preparation time: 1 hour > Cooking time: 12 minutes

INGREDIENTS

4 eggs

100 g/3½ oz caster sugar

75 g/2¾ oz self-raising flour

2 tbsp cocoa powder

ICING

150 g/5½ oz dark chocolate

2 egg yolks

150 ml/5 fl oz milk

125 g/4½ oz butter

50 g/1¼ oz icing sugar

2 tbsp rum, optional

TO DECORATE

a little white glacé or royal icing

icing sugar, to dust

holly or Christmas cake decorations

METHOD

1 Grease and line a 30 x 23-cm/12 x 9-inch Swiss roll tin.

2 Whisk the eggs and caster sugar in a bowl with electric beaters until the mixture is light and foamy and the whisk leaves a trail.

3 Sieve the flour and cocoa powder into the mixture and fold in. Pour into the prepared tin and bake in a preheated oven, 200°C/400°F/ Gas Mark 6, for 12 minutes, or until springy to the touch.

4 Turn out on to baking paper sprinkled with caster sugar. Peel off the lining paper and trim the edges. Cut a small slit halfway into the cake about 1 cm/½ inch from one short end. Starting at that end, roll up tightly, enclosing the paper. Place on a wire rack to cool.

5 To make the icing, melt the chocolate, beat in the egg yolks and milk, and heat, stirring, until the mixture thickens enough to coat the back of a wooden spoon. Cover with dampened greaseproof paper and cool.

6 Beat the butter and sugar until pale and fluffy. Beat in the custard and rum, if using.

7 Unroll the sponge, spread with one-third of the icing and roll up again. Place on a serving plate. Spread the remaining icing over the cake and mark with a fork to give the effect of bark. Leave to set. Pipe white icing to form the rings of the log. Sprinkle with sugar and decorate.

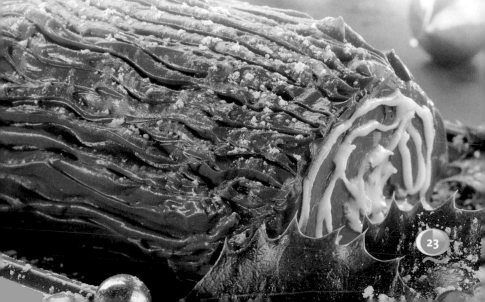

BANANA PROFITEROLES WITH CHOCOLATE SAUCE

>Serves 4–6   >Preparation time: 45 minutes   >Cooking time: 15–20 minutes

INGREDIENTS

CHOUX PASTRY

150 ml/5 fl oz water

55 g/2 oz butter

85 g/3 oz strong plain flour, sieved

2 eggs

CHOCOLATE SAUCE

100 g/3½ oz dark chocolate, broken into pieces

2 tbsp water

50 g/1¾ oz icing sugar

2 tbsp unsalted butter

FILLING

300 ml/10 fl oz double cream

1 banana

25 g/1 oz icing sugar

2 tbsp banana-flavoured liqueur

METHOD

1 Lightly grease a baking tray and sprinkle with a little water.

2 To make the pastry, place the water in a pan. Cut the butter into small pieces and add to the pan. Heat gently until the butter melts, then bring to a rolling boil.

3 Remove the pan from the heat and add the flour in one go, beating well until the mixture leaves the sides of the pan and forms a ball. Leave to cool slightly, then gradually beat in the eggs to form a smooth, glossy mixture. Spoon the paste into a large piping bag fitted with a 1-cm/½-inch plain nozzle.

4 Pipe about 18 small balls of the paste on to the baking tray, allowing enough room for them to expand during cooking. Bake in a preheated oven, 220°C/425°F/Gas Mark 7, for 15–20 minutes, until crisp and golden. Remove from the oven. Make a small slit in each one for steam to escape. Cool on a wire rack.

5 To make the sauce, place all the ingredients in a heatproof bowl, set over a pan of simmering water and heat, stirring, until well combined and smooth.

6 To make the filling, whip the cream until standing in soft peaks. Mash the banana with the sugar and liqueur. Fold into the cream. Place in a piping bag fitted with a 1-cm/½-inch plain nozzle and pipe into the profiteroles. Serve with the sauce poured over.

24

CHOCOLATE & RASPBERRY LAYER CAKE

> Serves 8–10   > Preparation time: 55 minutes   > Cooking time: 45–50 minutes

INGREDIENTS

150 ml/5 fl oz vegetable oil

150 ml/5 fl oz full-fat natural yogurt

175 g/6 oz light muscovado sugar

3 eggs, beaten

100 g/3½ oz wholemeal self-raising flour

125 g/4½ oz self-raising flour, sieved

2 tbsp cocoa powder

1 tsp bicarbonate of soda

50 g/1¾ oz dark chocolate, melted

FILLING AND TOPPING

150 ml/5 fl oz full-fat natural yogurt

150 ml/5 fl oz double cream

225 g/8 oz fresh soft fruit, such as strawberries or raspberries

METHOD

1 Grease a deep 23-cm/9-inch round cake tin and line the base with baking paper.

2 Place the oil, yogurt, sugar and beaten eggs in a large bowl and beat until well combined. Sieve the flours, cocoa powder and bicarbonate of soda together and beat into the bowl until well combined. Beat in the melted chocolate.

3 Pour into the prepared tin and bake in a preheated oven, 180°C/350°F/Gas Mark 4, for 45–50 minutes, or until a fine skewer inserted into the centre comes out clean. Leave to cool in the tin for 5 minutes, then turn out on to a wire rack to cool completely. When cold, split the cake into 3 layers.

4 To make the filling, place the yogurt and cream in a large mixing bowl and whisk well until the mixture stands in soft peaks.

5 Place one layer of cake on to a serving plate and spread with some of the cream. Top with some fruit (slicing the larger fruit). Repeat with the next layer. Top with the final cake layer and spread with the rest of the cream. Arrange more fruit on top. Cut into wedges to serve.

DARK & WHITE CHOCOLATE CHEESECAKE

>Serves 10–12   >Preparation time: 1½ hours   >Cooking time: 0 minutes

INGREDIENTS

BASE

225 g/8 oz toasted oat cereal

50 g/1¾ oz toasted hazelnuts, chopped

4 tbsp butter

25 g/1 oz dark chocolate

FILLING

350 g/12 oz full-fat soft cheese

100 g/3½ oz caster sugar

200 ml/7 fl oz thick yogurt

300 ml/10 fl oz double cream

1 sachet gelatine

3 tbsp water

175 g/6 oz dark chocolate, melted

175 g/6 oz white chocolate, melted

METHOD

1 Place the toasted oat cereal in a plastic bag and crush with a rolling pin. Pour the crushed cereal into a mixing bowl and stir in the chopped hazelnuts.

2 Melt the butter and chocolate together over a low heat and add to the cereal mixture, stirring until well coated.

3 Using the bottom of a glass, press the mixture into the base and up the sides of a 20-cm/8-inch springform tin.

4 To make the filling, beat together the cheese and sugar with a wooden spoon until smooth. Beat in the yogurt. Whip the cream until just holding its shape and fold into the mixture. Sprinkle the gelatine over the water in a heatproof bowl and leave to go spongy. Place over a pan of hot water and stir until dissolved. Stir into the mixture.

5 Divide the mixture in half and beat the dark chocolate into one half and the white chocolate into the other half.

6 Place alternate spoonfuls of mixture on top of the cereal base. Swirl the filling with the tip of a knife to give a marbled effect. Level the top. Chill until set before serving.

CLASSIC MISSISSIPPI MUD PIE

> Serves 8–10 > Preparation time: 2½ hours > Cooking time: 1 hour 10 minutes

INGREDIENTS

PASTRY

225 g/8 oz plain flour

25 g/1 oz cocoa powder

150 g/5½ oz butter

25 g/1 oz caster sugar

about 2 tbsp cold water

FILLING

175 g/6 oz butter

350 g/12 oz dark muscovado sugar

4 eggs, lightly beaten

4 tbsp cocoa powder, sieved

150 g/5½ oz dark chocolate

300 ml/10 fl oz single cream

1 tsp chocolate flavouring

425 ml/15 fl oz double cream, whipped

thick bar of chocolate

METHOD

1 To make the pastry, sieve the flour and cocoa powder into a mixing bowl. Rub in the butter until the mixture resembles fine breadcrumbs. Stir in the sugar and enough cold water to mix to a soft dough. Chill for 15 minutes.

2 Roll out the dough on a lightly floured surface and use to line a deep 23-cm/9-inch loose-bottomed flan tin or ceramic flan dish. Line with foil or baking paper and baking beans. Bake blind in a preheated oven, 190°C/375°F/Gas Mark 5, for 15 minutes. Remove the beans and foil or paper and cook for a further 10 minutes, or until crisp.

3 To make the filling, beat the butter and sugar in a bowl and gradually beat in the eggs with the cocoa powder. Melt the chocolate and beat it into the mixture with the single cream and the chocolate flavouring.

4 Pour the mixture into the cooked pastry case and bake at 160°C/325°F/Gas Mark 3 for 45 minutes, or until the filling is set.

5 Leave to cool completely, then transfer the pie to a serving plate, if preferred. Cover with the whipped cream and chill.

6 Use a potato peeler to remove curls from the bar of chocolate, scattering them over the pie. Chill before serving.

QUICK CHOCOLATE VANILLA FUDGE

›Makes 25–30 pieces ›Preparation time: 1¼ hours ›Cooking time: 5 minutes

INGREDIENTS

500 g/1 lb 2 oz dark chocolate

75 g/2¾ oz unsalted butter

400 ml/14 fl oz condensed milk

½ tsp vanilla essence

METHOD

1 Grease a 20-cm/8-inch square cake tin.

2 Break the chocolate into pieces and place in a large saucepan with the butter and milk.

3 Heat gently, stirring until the chocolate and butter melt and the mixture is smooth. Do not allow to boil.

4 Remove from the heat. Beat in the vanilla essence, then beat the mixture for a few minutes until thickened. Pour it into the prepared tin and level the top.

5 Chill in the refrigerator until firm.

6 Tip the fudge out on to a chopping board and cut into squares to serve.

CHOCOLATE MILK SHAKE & ICE CREAM SODA

> Serves 2 each   > Preparation time: 5 minutes each   > Cooking time: 0 minutes

CHOCOLATE MILK SHAKE

INGREDIENTS

450 ml/16 fl oz ice-cold milk

3 tbsp drinking chocolate powder

3 scoops chocolate ice cream

cocoa powder, to dust (optional)

METHOD

1 Place half of the ice-cold milk in a blender.

2 Add the drinking chocolate powder to the blender and 1 scoop of the chocolate ice cream. Blend until the mixture is frothy and well mixed. Stir in the remaining milk.

3 Place the remaining 2 scoops of chocolate ice cream in 2 serving glasses and carefully pour the chocolate milk over the ice cream.

4 Sprinkle a little cocoa powder, if using, over the top of each drink, and serve at once.

ICE CREAM SODA

INGREDIENTS

5 tbsp chocolate dessert sauce

soda water

2 scoops of chocolate ice cream

double cream, whipped (optional)

dark or milk chocolate, grated

METHOD

1 Divide the dessert sauce between 2 glasses.

2 Add a little soda water to each glass and stir to combine the sauce and soda water. Place a scoop of ice cream in each glass and top up with more soda water.

3 Place a dollop of whipped double cream on the top, if using, then sprinkle the cream with a little grated dark or milk chocolate.

CHOCOLATE RUM POTS

>Serves 6 >Preparation time: 2 hours 20 minutes >Cooking time: 5 minutes

INGREDIENTS

225 g/8 oz dark chocolate

4 eggs, separated

75 g/2³/₄ oz caster sugar

4 tbsp dark rum

4 tbsp double cream

CHOCOLATE SHAPES

a little melted white chocolate

a little melted dark chocolate

METHOD

1 Melt the chocolate and leave to cool slightly.

2 Whisk the egg yolks with the caster sugar in a bowl using electric beaters until very pale and fluffy.

3 Drizzle the chocolate into the mixture and fold in together with the rum and the cream.

4 Whisk the egg whites in a grease-free bowl until standing in soft peaks. Fold the egg whites into the chocolate mixture in 2 batches. Divide the mixture between 6 ramekins, or other individual dishes, and leave to chill for at least 2 hours.

5 Meanwhile, make the shapes for the decoration. Spoon the melted white chocolate into a paper pastry bag and snip off the tip. Spread some melted dark chocolate on a piece of baking paper. While still wet, pipe a fine line of white chocolate in a scribble over the top. Use the tip of a cocktail stick to marble the white chocolate into the dark. When firm but not too hard, cut into shapes with a small hand cutter or a sharp knife. Chill the shapes until firm, then use to decorate the desserts.

CHOCOLATE ALMOND TRUFFLES

>Makes about 24   >Preparation time: 50 minutes   >Cooking time: 5 minutes

INGREDIENTS

175 g/6 oz dark chocolate

2 tbsp almond-flavoured liqueur (amaretto) or orange-flavoured liqueur

40 g/1½ oz unsalted butter

50 g/1¾ oz icing sugar

50 g/1¾ oz ground almonds

50 g/1¾ oz grated chocolate

METHOD

1 Melt the dark chocolate with the liqueur, stirring until well combined.

2 Add the butter and stir until it has melted. Stir in the icing sugar and ground almonds.

3 Leave the mixture in a cool place until firm enough to roll into about 24 balls.

4 Place the grated chocolate on a plate and roll the truffles in the chocolate to coat them.

5 Place the truffles in paper sweet cases and chill in the refrigerator.

INDEX